This Book belongs to

· · · · · · · · · · · ·

Here's a Little

A Very First Book of

COLLECTED BY JANE YOLEN AND ANDREW FUSEK PETERS · ILLUSTRATED BY

To my grandchildren, all poetry lovers:
Glendon, Maddison, Alison, David, Caroline, and Amelia —J. Y.

To Asa, Olivia, and Madeleine —A. F. P.

For Elizabeth —P. D.

WALKER BOOKS
AND SUBSIDIARIES
LONDON ∘ BOSTON ∘ SYDNEY ∘ AUCKLAND

First published 2007 by Walker Books Ltd 87 Vauxhall Walk, London SE11 5HJ

10 9 8 7 6 5 4 3

Anthology Copyright © 2007 Jane Yolen and Andrew Fusek Peters
Poems © individual authors as noted in the acknowledgements
Illustrations © 2007 Polly Dunbar

The right of Polly Dunbar to be identified as illustrator of this work has been
asserted by her in accordance with the Copyright, Designs and Patents Act 1988

This book has been typeset in Kosmik

Printed in China

British Library Cataloguing in Publication Data: a catalogue record for this book is available from the British Library

ISBN-13: 978-1-84428-753-6

www.walkerbooks.co.uk

Poem
Poetry

POLLY DUNBAR

Here's a Little Foot

Here's a little foot.

What shall we do with it?

Me Myself and I

Lift it up

And into a shoe with it.

WENDY COPE

A Circle of Sun

I'm dancing.
I'm leaping.
I'm skipping about.
I gallop.
I grin.
I giggle.
I shout.
I'm Earth's many colors.
I'm morning and night.
I'm honey on toast.
I'm funny.
I'm bright.
I'm swinging.
I'm singing.
I wiggle.
I run.
I'm a piece of the sky
in a circle of sun.

REBECCA KAI DOTLICH

Something About Me

There's something about me

That I'm knowing.

There's something about me

That isn't showing.

I'm growing!

ANONYMOUS

I Am Rose

I am Rose my eyes are blue

I am Rose and who are you?

I am Rose and when I sing

I am Rose like anything.

GERTRUDE STEIN

Bananas and Cream

Bananas and cream,

Bananas and cream:

All we could say was

Bananas and cream.

We couldn't say fruit,

We couldn't say cow,

We didn't say sugar—

We don't say it now.

Bananas and cream,

Bananas and cream,

All we could shout was

Bananas and cream.

We didn't say why,

We didn't say how;

We forgot it was fruit,

We forgot the old cow;

We never said sugar,

We only said WOW!

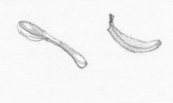

Bananas and cream,

Bananas and cream;

And all that we want is

Bananas and cream!

We didn't say dish,

We didn't say spoon;

We said not tomorrow,

But NOW and HOW SOON

Bananas and cream,

Bananas and cream?

We yelled for bananas,

Bananas and scream!

DAVID M^cCORD

Dressing Too Quickly

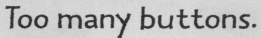

Too many buttons.

What a long zip.

Velcro to fasten.

Mind you don't slip.

Dress more slowly.

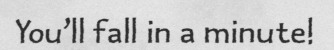

You'll fall in a minute!

You've one trouser leg

And two legs in it.

JILL TOWNSEND

Halfway Down

Halfway down the stairs

Is a stair

Where I sit.

There isn't any

Other stair

Quite like

It.

I'm not at the bottom,

I'm not at the top;

So this is the stair

Where

I always

Stop.

A. A. MILNE

Just Watch

Watch

how high

I'm jumping,

Watch

how far

I hop,

Watch

how long

I'm skipping,

Watch

how fast

I stop!

MYRA COHN LIVINGSTON

Jam on Toast

Why is strawberry jam so red?

Why is toast so brown?

Why when I drop it on the floor

Is it always jam side down?

GARETH OWEN

Soggy Greens

Oh, soggy greens, I hate you,

I hate your sloppy slush;

And if my mum would let me,

I'd throw you in a bush.

Oh, apple pie, I love you,

I love your crunchy crust;

And if my mum would let me,

I'd eat you till I bust.

JOHN CUNLIFFE

Baby Fingers

Baby fingers drum the crib.
Baby tugs the moon-white bib.

Baby fingers stir stewed pear.
Baby flings food everywhere.

Baby fingers toy with toes.
Baby rubs an itchy nose.

Baby fingers twirl Mom's hair.
Baby tickles Teddy Bear.

Baby fingers yank new grass.
Baby stuffs it in a glass.

Baby fingers sift the sand.
Baby pours some in Gram's hand.

Baby fingers poke this book.
Baby turns the pages. Look!

Baby fingers trace the sky.
Baby fingers wave. Bye-bye!

NIKKI GRIMES

Your Birthday Cake

Your birthday cake is made of mud

Because I cannot cook.

I cannot read a recipe or follow in a book.

I'm not allowed to use the stove

To simmer, roast, or bake.

I have no money of my own to buy a birthday cake.

I'm sure to get in trouble if I mess around with dough.

But I've made your birthday cake of mud

Because I love you so.

ROSEMARY WELLS

Baby in a High Chair

Baby in a high chair,
baby in a bib,
baby in a stroller,
baby in a crib.

Baby with the giggles,
baby with a smile,
such a lovely baby,
happy all the while.

JACK PRELUTSKY

Sugarcake Bubble

Sugarcake, sugarcake
Bubbling in a pot,
Bubble, bubble sugarcake
Bubble thick and hot.

24

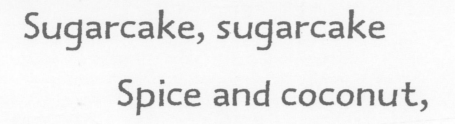

Sugarcake, sugarcake

Spice and coconut,

Sweet and sticky

Brown and gooey,

I could eat the lot.

GRACE NICHOLS

25

Candles

Three little candles
On a birthday cake.

Count them very carefully
So there's no mistake.

We counted three and there's no doubt—
Now it's time to blow them out.

WENDY COPE

Happy Birthday!

Happy Birthday to you!

Squashed tomatoes and stew!

Bread and butter

In the gutter

Happy Birthday to you!

TRADITIONAL BRITISH STREET RHYME

The NO-NO Bird

I'm the no-no bird,
That's right, that's me.
I live up in
The Tantrum Tree.

I'm the no-no bird,
I won't say why
I stamp my feet
And shout and cry.

I'm the no-no bird!
I sulk and sing
No! No! No!
To everything.

ANDREW FUSEK PETERS

28

Piggy Back

My daddy rides me piggy back.

My mama rides me, too.

But grandma says her poor old back

Has had enough to do.

LANGSTON HUGHES

Who Lives in My House?

Cat Kisses

Sandpaper kisses

On a cheek or a chin

That is the way

For a day to begin!

Sandpaper kisses

A cuddle, a purr.

I have an alarm clock

That's covered with fur.

BOBBI KATZ

Mum Is Having a Baby!

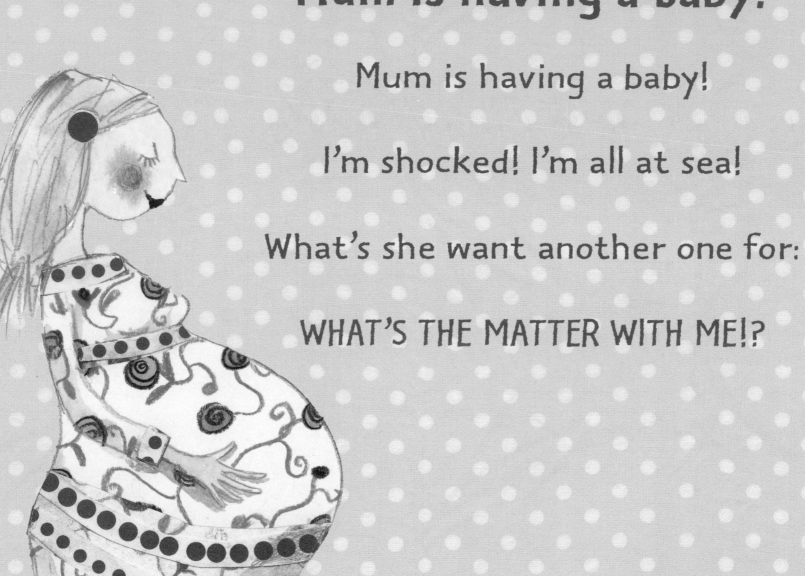

Mum is having a baby!

I'm shocked! I'm all at sea!

What's she want another one for:

WHAT'S THE MATTER WITH ME!?

COLIN McNAUGHTON

Chicks

Yesterday

They were warm, brown eggs.

Now they're fluffy, yellow balls

On legs.

ERIC FINNEY

My Puppy

It's funny

My puppy

Knows just how I feel.

When I'm happy,

He's yappy

And squirms like an eel!

When I'm grumpy,

He's slumpy

And stays at my heel.

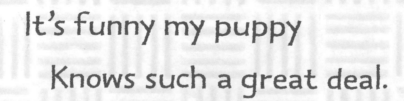

It's funny my puppy

Knows such a great deal.

AILEEN FISHER

Hamsters

Hamsters are the nicest things

That anyone could own.

I like them even better than

Some dogs that I have known.

Their fur is soft, their faces nice.

They're small when they are grown.

And they sit inside your pocket

When you are all alone.

MARCI RIDLON

Grandpa

Grandpa's hands are as rough as
Garden sacks
And as warm as pockets.
His skin is crushed paper round
His eyes
Wrapping up their secrets.

BERLIE DOHERTY

My Sister

My sister's remarkably light,

She can float to a fabulous height.

It's a troublesome thing,

But we tie her with string,

And we use her instead of a kite.

MARGARET MAHY

Ivy Says

The parade is passing

But I can't see

With the forest of legs

Surrounding me.

So up his trunk,

From the bough of his knee,

I climb my dad,

Who's as tall as a tree.

PHILIP WADDELL

43

Brother

I had a little brother
And brought him to my mother
And I said I want another
Little brother for a change.
But she said don't be a bother
So I took him to my father
And I said this little bother
Of a brother's very strange.

But he said one little brother
Is exactly like another
And every little brother
Misbehaves a bit he said.
So I took the little bother
From my mother and my father
And put the little bother
Of a brother back to bed.

MARY ANN HOBERMAN

45

The Older the Violin the Sweeter the Tune

Me granny old
Me granny wise
Stories shine like a moon
From inside she eyes.

Me granny can dance
Me granny can sing
But she can't play violin.

Yet she always saying,
"Dih older dih violin
de sweeter de tune."

Me granny must be wiser
Than the man in the moon.

JOHN AGARD

A Musical Family

I can play the piano.

I am nearly three.

I can play the long white note

That Mum calls Middle C.

Dad can play the clarinet.
My sister plays the fiddle.
But I'm the one who hits the piano
Slap bang in the middle.

JOHN MOLE

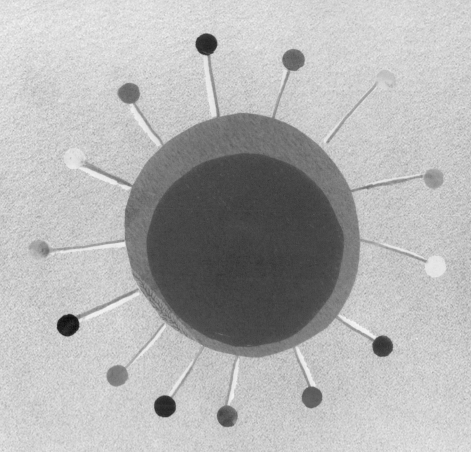

August Ice Cream Cone

Lick

Quick.

PAUL B. JANECZKO

I Go Outside

Ice Cream Cone

Strawberry ice cream
cold and sweet;
sugar cone
my favorite treat!

Pink and sticky
melting drips;
I lick it off
my finger tips!

HEIDI E. Y. STEMPLE

Recipe for Green

Take one seed,

Take one plot
Of deep, dark earth.
(But not a lot.)

Dig a bit,
Leave a while.

(More than a minute,
Less than a mile.)

Take some rain,
Take some sun;

Now your work is
Almost done.

Up from under,
Out from in,
Look out,
Sprout,

Time to begin.

JANE YOLEN

Berries

Hurry
Berry
Hurry!
Fatten in the sun.

Huckleberry
Gooseberry
Dribble-dribble
  juice berry
Raspberry
Hackberry
Nibble-nibble
  blackberry
Hurry
Everyone!

The way
Berries
Grow
Is
TOO
SLOW.

LILIAN MOORE

Bumble Bee

Black and yellow
Little fur bee
Buzzing away
In the timothy
Drowsy
Browsy
Lump of a bee
Rumbly
Tumbly
Bumbly bee.

Where are you taking
Your golden plunder
Humming along
Like baby thunder?
Over the clover
And over the hay
Then over the apple trees
Zoom away.

MARGARET WISE BROWN

Beach Time

We're driving to the beach now,

The air's potato chips—

so salty on my fingers,

so salty on my lips.

We're running on the beach now,

The waves play with the sea.

I wonder if I'm chasing them

or if they're chasing me.

We have to leave the beach now,

Good-bye sand and sun and foam.

But in my hand I hold a shell

to bring the beach back home.

MARILYN SINGER

Sand House

I built a house
One afternoon
With bucket, cup
And tablespoon.

Then scooped a shovel
Full of shore
On top to add
The second floor.

But when the fingers
Of the sea
Reached up and waved
A wave to me,

It tumbled down
Like dominoes
And disappeared
Between my toes.

J. PATRICK LEWIS

The Swing

How do you like to go up in a swing,
  Up in the air so blue?
    Oh, I do think it the pleasantest thing
     Ever a child can do.

     Up in the air and over the wall,
      Till I can see so wide,
       Rivers and trees and cattle and all
        Over the countryside—

        Till I look down on the garden green,
         Down on the roof so brown—
          Up in the air I go flying again,
           Up in the air and down.

ROBERT LOUIS STEVENSON

I'm Small

The wind is shaking every tree.
The wind is strong
But trees are tall.

The wind is pounding every wall.
But walls are strong
And they won't fall.

I think I'll hold on tight today
I'm small.

LILIAN MOORE

Kick a Little Stone

When you are walking by yourself

Here's something nice to do:

Kick a little stone and watch it

Hop ahead of you.

The little stone is round and white,

Its shadow round and blue.

Along the sidewalk over the cracks

The shadow bounces too.

DOROTHY ALDIS

Paper Songs

Launch a flimsy paper kite
In an autumn meadow;

If it tugs away in flight,
Trace it by its shadow.

Make a little paper boat,
Take it to the river;

If it swims and stays afloat,
You will live forever.

GERDA MAYER

Rain

There are holes in the sky
Where the rain gets in,
But they're ever so small
That's why rain is thin.

SPIKE MILLIGAN

April Rain Song

Let the rain kiss you.
Let the rain beat upon your head
   with silver liquid drops.
Let the rain sing you a lullaby.

The rain makes still pools on the sidewalk.
The rain makes running pools in the gutter.
The rain plays a little sleep-song
   on our roof at night—

And I love the rain.

LANGSTON HUGHES

Mud

Mud, mud, glorious mud,
Nothing quite like it for cooling
 the blood!
So follow me, follow
 Down to the hollow
And there let us wallow
 In glorious mud!

FLANDERS AND SWANN

Rickety Train Ride

I'm taking the train to Ricketywick
Clickety clickety clack.
I'm sat in my seat
With a sandwich to eat
As I travel the trickety track.

It's an ever so rickety trickety train,
And I honestly thickety think
That before it arrives
At the end of the line
It will tip up my drippety drink.

TONY MITTON

Tide and Seek

At night the stars fall out of bed,

For them the dark is day instead.

The moon is bright, it's time to play

Hide and seek with the Milky Way.

ANDREW FUSEK PETERS

After a Bath

After my bath
I try, try, try
to wipe myself
till I'm dry, dry, dry.

Hands to wipe
and fingers and toes
and two wet legs
and a shiny nose.

Just think how much
less time I'd take
if I were a dog
and could

shake, shake, shake.

AILEEN FISHER

Grandma's Lullaby

Close your eyes,
My precious love,
Grandma's little
Turtledove.

Go to sleep now,
Pretty kitty,
Grandma's little
Chickabiddy.

Stop your crying,
Cuddly cutie,
Grandma's little
Sweet patootie.

Issum, wissum,
Popsy wopsy,
Tootsie wootsie
Lollypopsie.
Diddims
Huggle
Snuggle pup

And now,
for Grandma's
sake, hush up!

CHARLOTTE POMERANTZ

Bed

In jumping and tumbling

We spend the whole day,

Till night by arriving

Has finished our play.

What then? One and all,

There's no more to be said,

As we tumbled all day,

So we tumble to bed.

ANONYMOUS

87

Night Bear

In the dark of night

when all is still

And I'm half-sleeping

in my bed;

It's good to know

my Teddy-bear

is snuggling

at my head.

LEE BENNETT HOPKINS

In Bed with Cuddly Creatures

Who's tucked up with me in bed?

Peter Panda
And Foxy Fred
Ally-Gator
Floppy Frog
Old Captain Hook
And Diddly Dog
Spotty Snake
And One-Armed Ted

All tucked up with me in bed.

WES MAGEE

Manhattan Lullaby

Lulled by rumble, babble, beep,
let these little children sleep;
let these city girls and boys
dream a music in the noise,
hear a tune their city plucks
up from buses, up from trucks
up from engines wailing *fire!*
up ten stories high, and higher,
up from hammers, rivets, drills,
up tall buildings, over sills,
up where city children sleep,
lulled by rumble, babble, beep.

NORMA FARBER

Late Last Night

Late last night
I lay in bed
Driving buses
In my head.

MICHAEL ROSEN

Sleepy Song

One wish to row your bed

Beyond the land of day,

One wish to blow your bed

Around the Bedtime Bay.

And one wish to float your bed

Where little dream birds play.

One wish to sway your bed

Above the sleepy tree.

One wish to sail your bed

Across the starry sea.

And one wish to bring you back

To morning time. And me.

CLARE BEVAN

Silverly

Silverly,

Silverly,

Over the

Trees,

The moon drifts

By on a

Runaway

Breeze.

Dozily,
Dozily,
Deep in her
Bed,
A little girl
Dreams with the
Moon in her
Head.

DENNIS LEE

Mrs Moon

Mrs Moon

Sitting up in the sky

Little old lady

Rock-a-bye

With a ball

Of fading light

And silvery needles

Knitting the night.

ROGER McGOUGH

You Be Saucer

You be saucer,
I'll be cup,
piggyback, piggyback,
pick me up.

You be tree,
I'll be pears,
carry me, carry me
up the stairs.

You be Good,
I'll be Night,
tuck me in, tuck me in
nice and tight.

EVE MERRIAM

Stargazing

Looking at the summer stars
   is our latest game.
I like to count them one by one
   while Dad gives each a name.

He says it's so much better
than trying to count sheep.
We make the stars our very own
before we fall asleep.

MARILYN SINGER

No Need to Light a Night-Light

You've no need to light a night-light
On a light night like tonight,
For a night-light's light's a slight light,
And tonight's a night that's light.

When a night's light, like tonight's light,
It is really not quite right
To light night-lights with their slight-lights
On a light night like tonight.

ANONYMOUS

Dream Maker

The shining silver moon

Is a coin hung in the sky

To pay the old Dream Maker

Whenever he goes by.

JANE YOLEN

The Early Morning

The moon on one hand, the dawn on the other:

The moon is my sister, the dawn is my brother.

The moon on my left and the dawn on my right.

My brother, good morning: my sister, good night!

HILAIRE BELLOC

As the Crow Flies

As the crow flies

As the river flows

As the sea gull cries

As the wind blows

As the eagle soars

As the frog leaps

As the lion roars

As the lamb sleeps

As the rabbit hops

As the owl calls

As the leaf drops

As the rain falls

As the turtle suns

As the snake slides

As the horse runs

As the swan glides

As the flower grows

As the willow sways

As the moon glows

As the wolf bays

As the rainbow arcs

As the sun burns

As the dog barks

As the earth turns

As the star gleams

As the doves coo

As the child dreams

So I love you.

LESLÉA NEWMAN

Index of Poems

Index of Poets